EASY OKRA COOKBOOK

RE-IMAGINE OKRA WITH 50 DELICIOUS OKRA RECIPES

By
BookSumo Press
Copyright © by Saxonberg Associates
All rights reserved

Published by
BookSumo Press, a DBA of Saxonberg Associates
http://www.booksumo.com/

About the Author.

BookSumo Press is a publisher of unique, easy, and healthy cookbooks.

Our cookbooks span all topics and all subjects. If you want a deep dive into the possibilities of cooking with any type of ingredient. Then BookSumo Press is your go to place for robust yet simple and delicious cookbooks and recipes. Whether you are looking for great tasting pressure cooker recipes or authentic ethic and cultural food. BookSumo Press has a delicious and easy cookbook for you.

With simple ingredients, and even simpler step-by-step instructions BookSumo cookbooks get everyone in the kitchen chefing delicious meals.

BookSumo is an independent publisher of books operating in the beautiful Garden State (NJ) and our team of chefs and kitchen experts are here to teach, eat, and be merry!

INTRODUCTION

Welcome to *The Effortless Chef Series*! Thank you for taking the time to purchase this cookbook.

Come take a journey into the delights of easy cooking. The point of this cookbook and all BookSumo Press cookbooks is to exemplify the effortless nature of cooking simply.

In this book we focus on Okra. You will find that even though the recipes are simple, the taste of the dishes are quite amazing.

So will you take an adventure in simple cooking? If the answer is yes please consult the table of contents to find the dishes you are most interested in.

Once you are ready, jump right in and start cooking.

— BookSumo Press

TABLE OF CONTENTS

About the Author 2

Introduction 3

Table of Contents 4

Any Issues? Contact Us 8

Legal Notes 9

Common Abbreviations 10

Chapter 1: Easy Okra Recipes 11

    Middle American Style Roasted Okra 11

    Southern Style Okra 13

    Crispy Lunch Box Okra Salad 15

    Okra from Afghanistan 18

    Summer-Time Charred Okra 20

    North Indian Inspired Curried Okra 22

    Barbados Style Okras 24

    Louisiana Okra 26

    Andhra Style Okra Stir-Fry 28

Southern Okra and Grits Fritters 30

South Carolina Inspired Deep Fried Okra 32

Okra Burgers 34

Baton Rouge Vegetarian Gumbo 36

Monday's Dinner 39

How to Cook Okra in the Oven 41

Acadian Dinner Okra 43

Canning Okra 45

Canning Okra II (Advanced) 47

Kuala Lampur Okra 50

Southern Hot Okra 52

Okra Lunch Salad 55

New Guinean Style Okra 58

Simply Okra 60

1980s Okra Classic 62

How to Make an Okra Stew 64

Middle Eastern Okra 66

Wednesday's Dinner 69

Southwestern Gumbo 71

Roxy's Okra Recipe 73

Okra Veggie Combination Platter	76
Homey Winter Casserole	78
Aunt Lexi's Dinner	80
Onondagan Inspired Okra	82
4-Ingredient Okra Skillet	84
Saturday's Creamy Okra	86
Curried Okra Classic	88
Okra Stew from the Orient	90
Authentic Punjabi Okra	93
Delish Indian Okra	95
Hearty Okra Soup	97
Red Café Stew	99
Mango Prawns and Coconut Okra	102
Rustic Road Tomato and Carrot Soup	105
Complex Mutton Stew	108
Egyptian Dinner	112
Asian Dream Okra Stir Fry	115
Jamaican Veggie Stew	118
Old-Fashioned Middle-Eastern Stew	121
A Filipino Dinner	124

Okra Veggie Combo 127

Stuffed Okra Sampler 130

THANKS FOR READING! JOIN THE CLUB AND KEEP ON COOKING WITH 6 MORE COOKBOOKS.... 132

Come On.. 134

Let's Be Friends :)... 134

Any Issues? Contact Us

If you find that something important to you is missing from this book please contact us at info@booksumo.com.

We will take your concerns into consideration when the 2nd edition of this book is published. And we will keep you updated!

— BookSumo Press

Legal Notes

ALL RIGHTS RESERVED. NO PART OF THIS BOOK MAY BE REPRODUCED OR TRANSMITTED IN ANY FORM OR BY ANY MEANS. PHOTOCOPYING, POSTING ONLINE, AND / OR DIGITAL COPYING IS STRICTLY PROHIBITED UNLESS WRITTEN PERMISSION IS GRANTED BY THE BOOK'S PUBLISHING COMPANY. LIMITED USE OF THE BOOK'S TEXT IS PERMITTED FOR USE IN REVIEWS WRITTEN FOR THE PUBLIC.

COMMON ABBREVIATIONS

cup(s)	C.
tablespoon	tbsp
teaspoon	tsp
ounce	oz.
pound	lb

*All units used are standard American measurements

Chapter 1: Easy Okra Recipes

Middle American Style Roasted Okra

Ingredients

- 18 fresh okra pods, sliced 1/3 inch thick
- 1 tbsp olive oil
- 2 tsp kosher salt
- 2 tsp black pepper

Directions

- Set your oven to 425 degrees F before doing anything else and line a baking sheet with a piece of the foil.
- Place the okra slices onto the prepared baking sheet in a single layer.
- Drizzle with the olive oil and sprinkle with the salt and pepper.
- Cook in the oven for about 10-15 minutes.

Amount per serving 3

Timing Information:

Preparation	5 m
Cooking	15 m
Total Time	20 m

Nutritional Information:

Calories	65 kcal
Fat	4.6 g
Carbohydrates	5.9g
Protein	1.6 g
Cholesterol	0 mg
Sodium	1286 mg

* Percent Daily Values are based on a 2,000 calorie diet.

Southern Style Okra

Ingredients

- 2 slices turkey bacon
- 1 lb. frozen okra, thawed and sliced
- 1 small onion, chopped
- 1/2 green bell pepper, chopped
- 2 celery, chopped
- 1 (14.5 oz.) can stewed tomatoes
- salt and pepper to taste

Directions

- Heat a large skillet on medium-high heat and cook the bacon till browned completely.
- Transfer the bacon onto a paper towel lined plate to drain and then crumble it.
- Discard the most of the bacon fat from the skillet, leaving a little inside.
- In the same skillet, add the okra, onion, pepper and celery and sauté till tender.
- Add the tomatoes, salt and pepper and cook till the tomatoes are heated completely.
- Serve with a topping of the crumbled bacon.

Amount per serving 6

Timing Information:

Preparation	10 m
Cooking	20 m
Total Time	30 m

Nutritional Information:

Calories	94 kcal
Fat	4.7 g
Carbohydrates	11.5g
Protein	3.8 g
Cholesterol	6 mg
Sodium	250 mg

* Percent Daily Values are based on a 2,000 calorie diet.

Crispy Lunch Box Okra Salad

Ingredients

- 3 slices bacon
- 1 (16 oz.) package frozen cut okra
- 1 onion, chopped
- 1 green bell pepper, seeded and diced
- 1 medium tomato, diced
- 1/3 C. white sugar
- 1/4 C. corn oil
- 1/4 C. white vinegar

Directions

- Heat a large skillet on medium heat and cook the bacon till browned completely.
- Transfer the bacon onto a paper towel lined plate to drain and then crumble it.
- Discard the most of the bacon fat from the skillet, leaving a little inside.
- In the same skillet, add the okra and fry for about 5 minutes.
- Transfer the okra to a salad bowl with the onion, green pepper, tomato and bacon and toss to coat.

- In a small bowl, add the sugar, corn oil and vinegar and beat till the sugar dissolves.
- Place the vinaigrette over the salad and toss to coat well.
- Refrigerate to chill for about 30 minutes before serving.

Amount per serving 6

Timing Information:

Preparation	15 m
Cooking	10 m
Total Time	25 m

Nutritional Information:

Calories	226 kcal
Fat	15.8 g
Carbohydrates	19.6g
Protein	3.4 g
Cholesterol	10 mg
Sodium	121 mg

* Percent Daily Values are based on a 2,000 calorie diet.

OKRA FROM AFGHANISTAN

Ingredients

- 2 tbsp vegetable oil
- 1 onion, thinly sliced
- 2 tbsp tomato paste
- 1 lb. okra, sliced in 1/4 inch pieces
- 1 tsp ground turmeric
- salt and black pepper to taste
- 2 C. water

Directions

- In a large skillet, heat the oil on medium-low heat and cook the onion for about 15 minutes, stirring occasionally.
- Add the tomato paste and cook, stirring continuously till no lumps remain.
- Add the okra, turmeric, salt, pepper and water and bring to a boil on high heat.
- Reduce the heat to medium-low and simmer for about 15-20 minutes.
- Season to taste with the salt and pepper if required.

Amount per serving 4

Timing Information:

Preparation	10 m
Cooking	35 m
Total Time	45 m

Nutritional Information:

Calories	127 kcal
Fat	7.1 g
Carbohydrates	15.2g
Protein	3.3 g
Cholesterol	0 mg
Sodium	176 mg

* Percent Daily Values are based on a 2,000 calorie diet.

Summer-Time Charred Okra

Ingredients

- 1 lb. fresh okra
- 1/4 C. melted butter
- 1/4 C. Cajun seasoning

Directions

- Set your grill for high heat and lightly, grease the grill grate.
- Coat the okra with the melted butter and then roll in the Cajun seasoning.
- Cook the okra on the grill for about 2 minutes per side.

Amount per serving 4

Timing Information:

Preparation	5 m
Cooking	5 m
Total Time	10 m

Nutritional Information:

Calories	156 kcal
Fat	12 g
Carbohydrates	11.4g
Protein	3 g
Cholesterol	31 mg
Sodium	1501 mg

* Percent Daily Values are based on a 2,000 calorie diet.

North Indian Inspired Curried Okra

Ingredients

- 1 lb. okra, ends trimmed, cut into 1/4-inch rounds
- 1 tbsp olive oil
- 1 tsp whole cumin seeds
- 1/2 tsp curry powder
- 1/2 tsp chickpea flour
- 1/2 tsp salt

Directions

- In a microwave safe plate, place the okra and microwave on High for about 3 minutes.
- In a large skillet, heat the oil on medium heat and sauté the cumin till it turns golden brown.
- Stir in the okra and cook for about 5 minutes.
- Gently, stir in the curry powder, chickpea flour and salt and cook for about 2 minutes.
- Serve immediately.

Amount per serving 4

Timing Information:

Preparation	5 m
Cooking	10 m
Total Time	15 m

Nutritional Information:

Calories	69 kcal
Fat	3.7 g
Carbohydrates	8.5g
Protein	2.4 g
Cholesterol	0 mg
Sodium	301 mg

* Percent Daily Values are based on a 2,000 calorie diet.

Barbados Style Okras

Ingredients

- 3 tbsp olive oil
- 1 large onion, thinly sliced
- 2 cloves garlic, minced
- 4 C. fresh okra, ends trimmed and halved lengthwise
- salt to taste
- ground black pepper to taste
- 1 lime, juiced

Directions

- In a large skillet, heat the oil on medium heat and sauté the onion and garlic for about 5 minutes.
- Stir in the okra, salt and pepper and increase the heat to high.
- Cook, stirring occasionally for about 10 minutes.
- Stir in the lime juice and cook for about 2 minutes.

Amount per serving 6

Timing Information:

Preparation	10 m
Cooking	15 m
Total Time	25 m

Nutritional Information:

Calories	96 kcal
Fat	6.9 g
Carbohydrates	8.6g
Protein	1.8 g
Cholesterol	0 mg
Sodium	7 mg

* Percent Daily Values are based on a 2,000 calorie diet.

Louisiana Okra

Ingredients

- 2 tbsp olive oil
- 1/2 large onion, chopped
- 2 cloves garlic, minced
- 1/2 green bell pepper, chopped
- 1 (16 oz.) can diced tomatoes in juice
- 3/8 tsp dried thyme
- 2 tbsp chopped fresh parsley
- 1/4 tsp cayenne pepper
- salt and pepper to taste
- 1 (16 oz.) package frozen cut okra

Directions

- In a large skillet, heat the oil on medium heat and sauté the onion and garlic till tender.
- Add the green pepper and cook and till tender.
- Drain the tomatoes, reserving juice.
- Stir in the skillet, add the tomatoes, thyme, parsley, cayenne, salt and pepper.
- Simmer for about 5 minutes on medium heat.
- Add the frozen okra and add the enough reserved juice of tomatoes to cover the bottom of the pan.
- Cook, covered for about 15 minutes.

Amount per serving 4

Timing Information:

Preparation	10 m
Cooking	30 m
Total Time	40 m

Nutritional Information:

Calories	133 kcal
Fat	7.2 g
Carbohydrates	14.2g
Protein	4 g
Cholesterol	0 mg
Sodium	184 mg

* Percent Daily Values are based on a 2,000 calorie diet.

Andhra Style Okra Stir-Fry

Ingredients

- 1 lb. fresh okra
- salt to taste
- 2 tsp chili powder
- 3 tbsp olive oil
- 1 pinch asafoetida powder
- 1/2 tsp brown mustard seeds

Directions

- Rinse the okra and cut head and tail end off of each okra.
- Chop the okra into small pieces.
- In a small bowl, mix together the okra, salt, chili powder and asafoetida powder.
- In a medium skillet, heat the oil on medium-high heat oil and sauté the black mustard seeds till they pop.
- Add the okra mixture into the skillet and cook, covered for about 10-15 minutes.
- Serve hot.

Amount per serving 2

Timing Information:

Preparation	10m
Cooking	15m
Total Time	25m

Nutritional Information:

Calories	262 kcal
Fat	21.1 g
Carbohydrates	18g
Protein	5.1 g
Cholesterol	0 mg
Sodium	45 mg

* Percent Daily Values are based on a 2,000 calorie diet.

SOUTHERN OKRA AND GRITS FRITTERS

Ingredients

- 2 lb. fresh okra, sliced in 1/8 inch pieces
- 1 large tomato, diced
- 1 onion, diced
- 6 packets instant grits
- 2 eggs, lightly beaten
- salt and black pepper to taste
- 1/2 C. oil for frying

Directions

- In a large bowl, mix together the okra, tomato and onion.
- Add the grits, eggs, salt and pepper and with your hands, mix till well combined.
- Make about 2 1/2-inch sized patties from the mixture.
- In a cast iron skillet, heat the oil on medium-high heat.
- Add the fritter and cook for about 5 minutes per side.
- Transfer the patties onto the paper towel lined plate to drain.
- Serve immediately.

Amount per serving 6

Timing Information:

Preparation	15 m
Cooking	10 m
Total Time	25 m

Nutritional Information:

Calories	196 kcal
Fat	4 g
Carbohydrates	35.7g
Protein	8 g
Cholesterol	62 mg
Sodium	343 mg

* Percent Daily Values are based on a 2,000 calorie diet.

South Carolina Inspired Deep Fried Okra

Ingredients

- 10 pods okra, sliced in 1/4 inch pieces
- 1 egg, beaten
- 1 C. cornmeal
- 1/4 tsp salt
- 1/4 tsp ground black pepper
- 1/2 C. vegetable oil

Directions

- In a small bowl, soak the okra in egg for about 5-10 minutes.
- In a bowl, mix together the cornmeal, salt and pepper.
- In a large skillet, heat the oil on medium-high heat.
- Coat the okra with the cornmeal mixture evenly.
- Stir in the okra in hot oil and stir continuously.
- Reduce the heat to medium when okra first starts to brown and cook till golden.
- Transfer the okra onto the paper towel lined plate to drain.

Amount per serving 4

Timing Information:

Preparation	15 m
Cooking	15 m
Total Time	30 m

Nutritional Information:

Calories	394 kcal
Fat	29.2 g
Carbohydrates	29g
Protein	4.7 g
Cholesterol	46 mg
Sodium	167 mg

* Percent Daily Values are based on a 2,000 calorie diet.

OKRA BURGERS

Ingredients

- 3 C. vegetable oil for frying
- 1 lb. okra, finely chopped
- 1 C. finely chopped onion
- 1 tsp salt
- 1/4 tsp pepper
- 1/2 C. water
- 1 egg
- 1/2 C. all-purpose flour
- 1 tsp baking powder
- 1/2 C. cornmeal

Directions

- In a large skillet, heat 1-inch of the oil to 375 degrees F.
- In a bowl, mix together the flour, baking powder and cornmeal.
- In a large bowl, mix together the okra, onion, salt, pepper, water and egg.
- Add the flour mixture into the okra mixture and stir to combine.
- Carefully, place the okra mixture by spoonfuls into the hot oil and fry for about 2 minutes per side.
- With a slotted spoon, transfer onto the paper towel lined plate to drain.

Amount per serving 6

Timing Information:

Preparation	20 m
Cooking	10 m
Total Time	30 m

Nutritional Information:

Calories	224 kcal
Fat	12.3 g
Carbohydrates	25.1g
Protein	4.8 g
Cholesterol	31 mg
Sodium	467 mg

* Percent Daily Values are based on a 2,000 calorie diet.

Baton Rouge Vegetarian Gumbo

Ingredients

- 1 tbsp vegetable oil
- 1 clove garlic, minced
- 1 medium onion, finely chopped
- 1 medium green bell pepper, finely chopped
- 1/2 (16 oz.) package frozen okra, thawed and sliced
- 8 oz. fresh mushrooms, sliced
- 1 (14.5 oz.) can diced tomatoes with juice
- 1 (6 oz.) can tomato paste
- 1/2 tsp file powder
- 2 bay leaves
- 1 tsp salt
- 1 tsp ground black pepper
- 2 tbsp vegetable oil
- 2 tbsp all-purpose flour

Directions

- In a large pan, heat 1 tbsp of the oil on medium heat and sauté the garlic, onion and green bell pepper till tender.
- Stir in the okra, mushrooms, and diced tomatoes with liquid, tomato paste, file powder, bay leaves, salt and pepper.
- Cook for about 40 minutes, stirring occasionally.

- In a medium skillet, heat 2 tbsp of the oil on medium heat.
- Slowly, add the flour, stirring continuously and cook till a golden brown roux is formed.
- Place the roux into the okra mixture and cook, stirring occasionally for about 5-10 minutes.

Amount per serving 8

Timing Information:

Preparation	15 m
Cooking	1 h
Total Time	1 h 15 m

Nutritional Information:

Calories	105 kcal
Fat	5.5 g
Carbohydrates	12.4g
Protein	3.2 g
Cholesterol	0 mg
Sodium	542 mg

* Percent Daily Values are based on a 2,000 calorie diet.

Monday's Dinner

Ingredients

- 1 lb. turkey bacon - cooked and crumbled
- 1 large onion, chopped
- 3 C. sliced fresh or frozen okra
- 1 (14.5 oz.) can chicken broth
- 1 C. uncooked rice
- 1 1/2 C. water

Directions

- Heat a large skillet on medium-high heat and cook the bacon till browned completely.
- Transfer the bacon onto a paper towel lined plate to drain and then crumble it.
- Drain the grease from the skillet, leaving a little inside.
- In the same skillet, add the onion on medium-high heat and sauté for about 3 minutes.
- Stir in the crumbled bacon, sliced okra and chicken broth.
- Reduce the heat and simmer for about 15 minutes.
- Stir in the rice and water and simmer, covered for about 20 minutes.

Amount per serving 6

Timing Information:

Preparation	15 m
Cooking	45 m
Total Time	1 h

Nutritional Information:

Calories	281 kcal
Fat	10.8 g
Carbohydrates	32.3g
Protein	13 g
Cholesterol	27 mg
Sodium	583 mg

* Percent Daily Values are based on a 2,000 calorie diet.

How to Cook Okra in the Oven

Ingredients

- 1/2 lb. fresh okra, cut into 1/2 inch slices
- 8 cherry tomatoes, halved
- olive oil
- kosher salt and ground black pepper to taste
- garlic powder to taste
- 1/2 C. panko bread crumbs

Directions

- Set your oven to 425 degrees F before doing anything else and lightly, grease a baking sheet.
- In a bowl, add the okra, tomatoes, kosher salt, pepper and garlic powder and stir till the vegetables are coated with oil.
- Add the bread crumbs and stir to combine.
- Spread the vegetables onto the prepared baking sheet.
- Cook in the oven for about 13-15 minutes.

Amount per serving 2

Timing Information:

Preparation	5 m
Cooking	15 m
Total Time	20 m

Nutritional Information:

Calories	179 kcal
Fat	8 g
Carbohydrates	30.2g
Protein	5.8 g
Cholesterol	0 mg
Sodium	347 mg

* Percent Daily Values are based on a 2,000 calorie diet.

Acadian Dinner Okra

Ingredients

- 2 tbsp butter
- 2 tbsp olive oil
- 4 stalks celery, chopped
- 2 onions, chopped
- 4 ears fresh corn, shucked and kernels scraped from cob
- 2 lb. fresh okra, cut into 1/2 inch slices
- 2 (28 oz.) cans whole tomatoes, broken up
- 1/2 lb. andouille sausage, diced
- 1/2 tsp Creole seasoning
- sea salt and ground black pepper to taste

Directions

- In a large span, heat the oil on medium heat and sauté the celery and onions for about 5 minutes.
- Stir in the corn kernels and cook for about 3 minutes.
- Stir in the okra, tomatoes, andouille sausage and Creole seasoning and cook, covered for about 45 minutes.
- Season with sea salt, black pepper and more Creole seasoning if required and cook, uncovered for about 10 minutes.

Amount per serving 12

Timing Information:

Preparation	20 m
Cooking	1 h
Total Time	1 h 20 m

Nutritional Information:

Calories	180 kcal
Fat	10.4 g
Carbohydrates	19.1g
Protein	6.2 g
Cholesterol	16 mg
Sodium	436 mg

* Percent Daily Values are based on a 2,000 calorie diet.

CANNING OKRA

Ingredients

- 1 1/2 lb. fresh okra
- 3 dried red chili peppers
- 3 tsp dried dill
- 2 C. water
- 1 C. vinegar
- 2 tbsp salt

Directions

- Divide the fresh okra in 3 (1 pint) sterile jars evenly.
- Place one dried chili and 1 tsp of the dill into each jar.
- In a small pan, mix together the water, vinegar and salt and bring to a rolling boil.
- Pour the boiling mixture over the ingredients in the jars and seal.
- Process in a hot water bath for about 10 minutes.
- Refrigerate the jars after opening.

Amount per serving 24

Timing Information:

Preparation	1 h
Total Time	1 h

Nutritional Information:

Calories	10 kcal
Fat	< 0 g
Carbohydrates	< 2.1g
Protein	< 0.6 g
Cholesterol	0 mg
Sodium	585 mg

* Percent Daily Values are based on a 2,000 calorie diet.

CANNING OKRA II (ADVANCED)

Ingredients

- 1 quart white vinegar
- 1 1/3 C. water
- 1/3 C. salt
- 3 lb. small okra, stems trimmed
- 6 whole chili peppers
- 6 cloves garlic, peeled
- 1 tbsp mustard seed
- 6 (1 pint) sterilized canning jars with lids and rings

Directions

- In a pan, add the vinegar, water and salt on medium-high heat and bring to a boil.
- Remove from the heat.
- Sterilize the jars and lids in the boiling water for at least for about 5 minutes.
- In each hot, sterilized jars, pack the okra with 1 pepper and 1 garlic clove tightly.
- Sprinkle with the mustard seeds and place the vinegar mixture, leaving 1/2-inch space at the top.

- With a moist paper towel, wipe the rims of the jars to remove any food residue. Top with lids and screw on rings.
- Arrange a rack in the bottom of a large pan, filled halfway with the water and bring to a boil.
- Carefully with a holder, lower the jars into the boiling water, leaving a 2-inch space between the jars.
- Pour in more boiling water if necessary to bring the water level to at least 1 inch above the tops of the jars.
- Bring the water to a rolling boil and process, covered for about 10 minutes.
- Remove the jars from the pan and place onto a wood surface, several inches apart to cool completely.
- After cooling, press the top of each lid with a finger, ensuring that the seal is tight.
- Store in a cool, dark area for at least 4 weeks before opening.

Amount per serving 72

Timing Information:

Preparation	40 m
Cooking	20 m
Total Time	28 d 1 h

Nutritional Information:

Calories	9 kcal
Fat	< 0.1 g
Carbohydrates	< 1.8g
Protein	< 0.5 g
Cholesterol	0 mg
Sodium	519 mg

* Percent Daily Values are based on a 2,000 calorie diet.

Kuala Lampur Okra

Ingredients

- 1 tbsp vegetable oil
- 5 cloves garlic, minced
- 5 fresh red chili peppers, chopped
- 10 uncooked shrimp - peeled, deveined, and cut in half
- 10 fresh okra pods, sliced diagonally
- 1 tsp belachan (Malaysian chili-shrimp paste)
- 2 tsp light soy sauce
- 2 tbsp water

Directions

- In a skillet, heat the vegetable oil on medium-high heat and sauté the garlic for about 1 minute.
- Stir in the red chilies, shrimp, okra and belachan and cook for about 2 minutes.
- Add the light soy sauce and water and cook for about 2-4 more minutes.

Amount per serving 4

Timing Information:

Preparation	20 m
Cooking	10 m
Total Time	30 m

Nutritional Information:

Calories	97 kcal
Fat	4.1 g
Carbohydrates	9.2g
Protein	7 g
Cholesterol	38 mg
Sodium	205 mg

* Percent Daily Values are based on a 2,000 calorie diet.

Southern Hot Okra

Ingredients

- 1 lb. okra, sliced into 1/2-inch pieces
- 1 onion, chopped
- 1 large green tomato, diced
- 1 jalapeno pepper, seeded and minced
- 1 clove garlic, minced
- 1/2 C. milk
- 2 eggs, beaten
- 1/4 tsp salt
- 1/4 tsp ground black pepper
- 1 C. cornmeal
- 1/4 C. vegetable oil

Directions

- In a large bowl, mix together the okra, onion, green tomato, jalapeño pepper and garlic.
- In another bowl, add the milk, eggs, salt and black pepper and beat till well combined.
- Place the egg mixture over the vegetable mixture and toss to coat.

- Slowly, add the cornmeal into the vegetable mixture and mix till the liquid is absorbed and ingredients are moist evenly.
- In a skillet, heat the oil on medium heat.
- Add the vegetable mixture into the skillet and reduce the heat to medium-low.
- Cover and fry for about 10-15 minutes.
- Flip the fritter and fry for about 5-8 minutes.
- Cut into the slices and serve.

Amount per serving 6

Timing Information:

Preparation	30 m
Cooking	15 m
Total Time	45 m

Nutritional Information:

Calories	166 kcal
Fat	3.5 g
Carbohydrates	28.2g
Protein	6.6 g
Cholesterol	64 mg
Sodium	141 mg

* Percent Daily Values are based on a 2,000 calorie diet.

Okra Lunch Salad

Ingredients

- 2 slices bacon (optional)
- 2 (10 oz.) packages breaded frozen okra
- 1/3 C. chopped tomato
- 2 tbsp chopped green onion
- 2 tbsp chopped green bell pepper
- 1/2 C. vegetable oil
- 1/2 C. white sugar
- 1/4 C. distilled white vinegar

Directions

- Heat a large skillet on medium-high heat and cook the bacon till browned completely.
- Transfer the bacon onto a paper towel lined plate to drain and then crumble it.
- In the same skillet, add the okra and cook for about 10-15 minutes.
- Transfer the okra onto a paper towel lined plate to drain
- In a bowl, mix together the bacon, okra, tomato, green onion and green bell pepper.
- In a microwave-safe bowl, add the oil, sugar and vinegar and beat till combined.

- Microwave on High for about 1 minute, stirring after every 10 seconds.
- Place the dressing over the vegetables just before serving and toss to coat.

Amount per serving 6

Timing Information:

Preparation	20 m
Cooking	20 m
Total Time	40 m

Nutritional Information:

Calories	267 kcal
Fat	19.7 g
Carbohydrates	22.1g
Protein	3.2 g
Cholesterol	3 mg
Sodium	76 mg

* Percent Daily Values are based on a 2,000 calorie diet.

New Guinean Style Okra

Ingredients

- 1/2 lb. frozen whole okra
- 1 serrano pepper, chopped
- 2 cloves garlic, roughly chopped
- 1 tbsp lemon juice
- 1/2 tsp salt

Directions

- In a large pan of boiling water, boil the okra on high heat for about 8 minutes.
- Set a colander in the sink.
- Drain the okra in the colander completely.
- Trim the stems off the okra.
- In a food processor, add the trimmed okra, chili pepper, garlic, lemon juice and salt and pulse till smooth.

Amount per serving 8

Timing Information:

Preparation	5 m
Cooking	8 m
Total Time	13 m

Nutritional Information:

Calories	10 kcal
Fat	< 0.1 g
Carbohydrates	< 2.3g
Protein	< 0.5 g
Cholesterol	0 mg
Sodium	146 mg

* Percent Daily Values are based on a 2,000 calorie diet.

SIMPLY OKRA

Ingredients

- cooking spray
- 1 lb. fresh okra
- 1/4 C. canola oil
- 1 tsp garlic powder
- 1/2 tsp salt
- 1/4 tsp ground black pepper

Directions

- Set your grill for medium heat and lightly, grease the grill grate.
- Grease a grill basket with the cooking spray.
- Trim stem ends of the okra close to the top without piercing the pods and transfer into a large bowl.
- Add the canola, garlic powder, salt and pepper and toss to coat.
- Spread okra into the prepared grill basket.
- Cook on the grill for about 4-6 minutes, stirring occasionally.

Amount per serving 6

Timing Information:

Preparation	10 m
Cooking	5 m
Total Time	15 m

Nutritional Information:

Calories	108 kcal
Fat	9.4 g
Carbohydrates	5.7g
Protein	1.6 g
Cholesterol	0 mg
Sodium	201 mg

* Percent Daily Values are based on a 2,000 calorie diet.

1980s Okra Classic

Ingredients

- 2 slices turkey bacon, chopped
- 1 medium onion, chopped
- 1 (10 oz.) package frozen cut okra
- 1 (14.5 oz.) can diced tomatoes, drained
- 1 (20 oz.) package frozen corn
- 1 tbsp file powder
- salt and pepper to taste

Directions

- Heat a large skillet on medium-high heat and cook the bacon till it releases some of the juices.
- Add the onion and okra and fry till tender and browned, stirring continuously.
- Reduce the heat to medium.
- Add the tomatoes and simmer for about 20 minutes.
- Stir in the corn and simmer for another 10 minutes.
- Season with the file powder, salt and pepper and serve.

Amount per serving 6

Timing Information:

Preparation	15m
Cooking	25m
Total Time	40m

Nutritional Information:

Calories	167 kcal
Fat	5.3 g
Carbohydrates	27.8g
Protein	5.6 g
Cholesterol	6 mg
Sodium	189 mg

* Percent Daily Values are based on a 2,000 calorie diet.

How to Make an Okra Stew

Ingredients

- 1 lb. medium shrimp - peeled and deveined
- 1/2 lime, juiced
- 4 tbsp margarine
- 2 green bell peppers, seeded
- 6 tbsp minced shallots
- 1 C. frozen corn kernels
- 1 C. chopped okra
- 3 tomatoes - blanched, peeled and chopped
- 1 tbsp tomato paste
- 1/4 tsp dried thyme
- 1 bay leaf
- salt and pepper to taste
- 1 green chili pepper

Directions

- In a bowl, place the shrimp with lime juice and stir to coat.
- In a soup pan, melt the butter and sauté the green pepper and shallots for about 2-3 minutes.
- Stir in the corn, okra, tomatoes, tomato paste, thyme, bay leaf, chili pepper, salt and pepper and simmer for about 10 minutes.
- Add the shrimp and bring to a gentle boil and simmer for about 5 minutes.
- Discard the bay leaf and chili before serving.

Amount per serving 4

Timing Information:

Preparation	10m
Cooking	10m
Total Time	20m

Nutritional Information:

Calories	309 kcal
Fat	13.3 g
Carbohydrates	23.1g
Protein	27.1 g
Cholesterol	173 mg
Sodium	337 mg

* Percent Daily Values are based on a 2,000 calorie diet.

Middle Eastern Okra

Ingredients

- 2/3 C. olive oil
- 1 tbsp salt
- 1 lb. beef top sirloin, cut into 1-inch cubes
- 1/2 large onion, chopped
- 6 cloves garlic, minced
- 2 (10 oz.) cans tomato sauce
- 1 tbsp tomato paste
- 1 (10 oz.) package frozen okra, thawed
- 2 C. water
- 1 1/2 tbsp ground coriander
- 1 tsp ground white pepper
- 2 tsp ground cumin
- salt to taste
- 1 jalapeno pepper, thinly sliced

Directions

- Season the steak cubes with 1 tbsp of the salt.
- In a large pan, heat the oil on high heat and sear the steak cubes, onion and garlic for about 5 minutes.
- Reduce the heat to medium and cook for about 3 minutes.
- Transfer the steak cubes into a bowl and keep aside.

- Stir in the tomato sauce, tomato paste, okra, water, coriander, white pepper and cumin. And bring to a boil.
- Reduce the heat to low and simmer for about 30-45 minutes.
- Stir in the beef cubes and simmer for about 10 minutes.
- Serve with a garnishing of jalapeño slices.

Amount per serving 6

Timing Information:

Preparation	20 m
Cooking	50 m
Total Time	1 h 10 m

Nutritional Information:

Calories	366 kcal
Fat	29.1 g
Carbohydrates	12.4g
Protein	16 g
Cholesterol	33 mg
Sodium	1707 mg

* Percent Daily Values are based on a 2,000 calorie diet.

Wednesday's Dinner

Ingredients

- 7 C. water
- 1 lb. dried baby lima beans (butter beans)
- 1 lb. pickled pork shoulder, cubed, optional
- 1 onion, chopped
- 1 tbsp minced garlic
- 1/4 C. butter
- salt and pepper to taste
- 1 (10 oz.) package frozen cut okra

Directions

- In a soup pan, mix together the water, butter beans, pork, onion and garlic on medium heat and bring to a boil.
- Stir in the butter, salt and pepper and boil for about 20 minutes.
- Stir in the okra and cook for about 10 minutes.

Amount per serving 8

Timing Information:

Preparation	5 m
Cooking	1 h
Total Time	1 h 5 m

Nutritional Information:

Calories	331 kcal
Fat	11.7 g
Carbohydrates	39.5g
Protein	18.4 g
Cholesterol	38 mg
Sodium	67 mg

* Percent Daily Values are based on a 2,000 calorie diet.

Southwestern Gumbo

Ingredients

- 6 slices bacon, cut into 1 inch pieces
- 1 onion, diced
- 4 skinless, boneless chicken breast halves - cut into 1 inch cubes
- 2 (16 oz.) packages frozen cut okra
- 10 fresh cayenne peppers, chopped (optional)
- 1 (14.5 oz.) can diced tomatoes with juice
- 2 (10 oz.) cans diced tomatoes with green chili peppers
- 1 C. long grain white rice
- 3 C. water

Directions

- Heat a large Dutch oven on medium-high heat and cook the bacon till browned completely.
- Add the onion, chicken cubes and okra and stir fry for about 15 minutes.
- Stir in the cayenne peppers, tomatoes, and diced tomatoes with green chilies, rice and water and reduce the heat to medium-low.
- Simmer for about 20 minutes.

Amount per serving 12

Timing Information:

Preparation	30 m
Cooking	40 m
Total Time	1 h 10 m

Nutritional Information:

Calories	186 kcal
Fat	3.7 g
Carbohydrates	24.5g
Protein	14.3 g
Cholesterol	29 mg
Sodium	376 mg

* Percent Daily Values are based on a 2,000 calorie diet.

Roxy's Okra Recipe

Ingredients

- 1 (16 oz.) package frozen cut okra
- butter flavored cooking spray
- 1/4 C. yellow cornmeal
- 1/4 C. panko bread crumbs
- 1/2 tsp garlic salt
- 1/4 tsp ground black pepper (optional)

Directions

- Set your oven to 375 degrees F before doing anything else and arrange a baking rack into a sheet pan.
- In a microwave safe plate, place the frozen okra and microwave on High for about 8 minutes.
- Drain and place onto paper towel lined plate to cool for about 5-10 minutes.
- Spray the okra with the butter flavored cooking spray generously.
- In a plastic food storage bag, add the cornmeal, panko bread crumbs, garlic salt and pepper.
- Add the okra and shake to coat with the cornmeal mixture evenly.

- Remove the okra from the bag and place onto the baking rack over the sheet pan in a single layer.
- Cook under the broiler for about 15-20 minutes.

Amount per serving 4

Timing Information:

Preparation	10 m
Cooking	25 m
Total Time	35 m

Nutritional Information:

Calories	95 kcal
Fat	2 g
Carbohydrates	19.1g
Protein	3.3 g
Cholesterol	0 mg
Sodium	264 mg

* Percent Daily Values are based on a 2,000 calorie diet.

OKRA VEGGIE COMBINATION PLATTER

Ingredients

- 20 pods okra, sliced in 1/4 inch pieces
- 6 Yukon Gold potatoes, cut into 1-inch pieces
- 2 large sweet onion, cut into 1 inch pieces
- 1 (8.5 oz.) package corn bread mix (such as Jiffy(R))
- 1 C. vegetable oil for frying

Directions

- I a colander, place the vegetables and rinse under the cold water.
- Transfer the vegetables into a large bowl.
- Add enough corn meal and gently toss to coat completely.
- In a large frying pan, add enough oil to cover bottom and heat on medium to medium-high heat.
- Place the vegetables in batches in a single layer and cook till golden brown.
- Flip and cook till browned from the other side.
- Transfer the vegetable mixture onto a paper towel lined plate to drain.
- Repeat with the remaining vegetables.

Amount per serving 8

Timing Information:

Preparation	20 m
Cooking	45 m
Total Time	1 h 5 m

Nutritional Information:

Calories	236 kcal
Fat	5.8 g
Carbohydrates	41.9g
Protein	5.3 g
Cholesterol	< 1 mg
Sodium	< 489 mg

* Percent Daily Values are based on a 2,000 calorie diet.

Homey Winter Casserole

Ingredients

- 2 C. uncooked white rice
- 1 (3 lb.) whole chicken, cut into pieces
- 2 (28 oz.) cans whole peeled tomatoes, chopped, juice reserved
- 2 C. small fresh okra
- 2 bay leaves
- 5 C. chicken broth
- salt and black pepper to taste

Directions

- Set your oven to 350 degrees F before doing anything else.
- In the bottom of a 10x15-inch baking dish, spread the rice evenly.
- Top with the chicken pieces, followed by the tomatoes, okra, and bay leaves.
- Place the broth and reserved tomato juice and season with the salt and pepper.
- Cook in the oven, covered for about 2 hours.
- Discard the bay leaves before serving.

Amount per serving 10

Timing Information:

Preparation	10 m
Cooking	2 h
Total Time	2 h 10 m

Nutritional Information:

Calories	348 kcal
Fat	10.8 g
Carbohydrates	39g
Protein	23 g
Cholesterol	58 mg
Sodium	322 mg

* Percent Daily Values are based on a 2,000 calorie diet.

Aunt Lexi's Dinner

Ingredients

- 2 lb. medium shrimp - peeled and deveined
- salt and pepper to taste
- cayenne pepper to taste
- 1/2 C. olive oil
- 2 lb. chopped okra
- 1 tbsp tomato paste
- 1 tomato, chopped
- 1 C. chopped onion
- 4 cloves garlic, minced
- 1/2 C. chopped celery
- 1/2 C. chopped green bell pepper
- 12 C. water
- 1/2 C. chopped green onions

Directions

- Season the shrimp with the salt, pepper and cayenne and keep aside.
- In a large pan, heat the oil on medium heat and cook the okra for about 30 minutes, stirring occasionally.
- Add the tomato paste, tomato, onion, garlic, celery and green bell pepper and cook for about 15 minutes.
- Add the water and season to taste and bring to a boil.
- Reduce the heat to low and simmer for about 45 minutes.
- Stir in the shrimp and simmer for about 20 more minutes.
- Stir in the green onion and serve.

Amount per serving 6

Timing Information:

Preparation	15 m
Cooking	2 h
Total Time	2 h 15 m

Nutritional Information:

Calories	394 kcal
Fat	20.9 g
Carbohydrates	18.1g
Protein	34.8 g
Cholesterol	230 mg
Sodium	270 mg

* Percent Daily Values are based on a 2,000 calorie diet.

Onondagan Inspired Okra

Ingredients

- 3 tbsp butter
- 1 medium onion, chopped
- 1 lb. sliced fresh okra
- 1/2 tsp ground cumin
- 1/2 tsp ground ginger
- 1/2 tsp ground coriander
- 1/4 tsp ground black pepper
- salt to taste

Directions

- In a large skillet, melt the butter on medium heat and sauté the onion till tender.
- Stir in the okra, cumin, ginger, coriander, pepper and salt and sauté for a few minutes.
- Reduce the heat to medium-low and cook, covered for about 20 minutes, stirring occasionally.

Amount per serving 4

Timing Information:

Preparation	10 m
Cooking	25 m
Total Time	35 m

Nutritional Information:

Calories	126 kcal
Fat	8.9 g
Carbohydrates	11.1g
Protein	2.8 g
Cholesterol	23 mg
Sodium	169 mg

* Percent Daily Values are based on a 2,000 calorie diet.

4-Ingredient Okra Skillet

Ingredients

- 1 tbsp butter
- 3 onions, sliced
- 1 lb. fresh okra, sliced in 1/8 inch pieces
- 1 1/2 tsp ground turmeric

Directions

- In a medium frying pan, melt the butter on medium heat and sauté the onion till tender.
- Stir in the okra and turmeric and reduce heat to low.
- Simmer for about 15 minutes.

Amount per serving 8

Timing Information:

Preparation	5 m
Cooking	15 m
Total Time	20 m

Nutritional Information:

Calories	44 kcal
Fat	1.7 g
Carbohydrates	6.6g
Protein	1.7 g
Cholesterol	4 mg
Sodium	15 mg

* Percent Daily Values are based on a 2,000 calorie diet.

Saturday's Creamy Okra

Ingredients

- 1 (10.75 oz.) can condensed cream of mushroom soup
- 1 C. water (For creamier rice, increase the water amount to 1 1/3 C.)
- 3/4 C. uncooked brown rice
- 1/4 tsp paprika
- 1/4 tbsp ground black pepper
- 4 skinless, boneless chicken breasts
- 1 (16 oz.) package frozen okra, thawed and sliced

Directions

- Set your oven to 375 degrees F before doing anything else.
- In a 13x9-inch baking dish, mix together the soup, water, rice, okra, paprika and ground black pepper and top with the chicken.
- Sprinkle with the additional paprika and ground black pepper evenly.
- Cover and cook in the oven for about 45 minutes.

Amount per serving 5

Timing Information:

Preparation	15m
Cooking	45m
Total Time	1h

Nutritional Information:

Calories	287 kcal
Fat	5.8 g
Carbohydrates	32g
Protein	26.5 g
Cholesterol	55 mg
Sodium	459 mg

* Percent Daily Values are based on a 2,000 calorie diet.

CURRIED OKRA CLASSIC

Ingredients

- 4 C. okra, cut into 1-inch pieces
- 1 tbsp olive oil
- 1 tsp cumin seeds
- 1 onion, chopped
- 2 tomatoes, diced
- 1 tsp curry powder
- 1 tsp salt

Directions

- In a large, microwave-safe dish, place the okra and microwave on High for about 6 minutes.
- In a large skillet, heat the olive oil and cumin seeds on medium heat till the cumin seeds becomes golden brown.
- Add the onions and sauté for about 3 minutes.
- Add the tomatoes and cook for about 3 minutes.
- Stir in the okra, curry powder and salt and cook and for about 3 minutes more.
- Serve hot.

Amount per serving 4

Timing Information:

Preparation	20 m
Cooking	15 m
Total Time	35 m

Nutritional Information:

Calories	100 kcal
Fat	3.9 g
Carbohydrates	15.8g
Protein	3.4 g
Cholesterol	0 mg
Sodium	597 mg

* Percent Daily Values are based on a 2,000 calorie diet.

Okra Stew from the Orient

Ingredients

- 2 tbsp vegetable oil
- 2 large onions, chopped
- salt and ground black pepper to taste
- 2 lb. cubed lamb stew meat
- 3 tbsp ground cinnamon
- 1 1/2 tsp ground cumin
- 1 1/2 tsp ground coriander
- 1 1/2 tbsp garlic paste
- 5 (14.5 oz.) cans canned diced tomatoes, drained
- 1 1/2 tbsp tomato paste
- 2 beef bouillon cubes
- 4 C. boiling water
- 2 lb. frozen sliced okra

Directions

- In a large pan, heat the oil on medium heat and sauté the onion and black pepper for about 10 minutes.
- Add the lamb, cinnamon, cumin, coriander, and garlic paste and cook for about 10-15 minutes, stirring occasionally.
- Stir in the tomatoes and tomato paste and cook for about 5 minutes.
- In a heatproof bowl, dissolve the beef bouillon cubes in 4 C. of the boiling water.

- Add the boiling water mixture into the pan with the lamb, okra and water if required to cover the mixture and simmer, covered for about 30 minutes, stirring occasionally.
- Uncover and simmer for about 45-60 minutes.

Amount per serving 8

Timing Information:

Preparation	20 m
Cooking	2 h
Total Time	2 h 20 m

Nutritional Information:

Calories	262 kcal
Fat	8.3 g
Carbohydrates	22.6g
Protein	21.6 g
Cholesterol	53 mg
Sodium	779 mg

* Percent Daily Values are based on a 2,000 calorie diet.

Authentic Punjabi Okra

Ingredients

- 1/3 C. vegetable oil
- 1/4 tsp mustard seeds
- 1 pinch asafoetida powder
- 1 medium onion, thinly sliced
- 1 clove garlic, peeled and sliced
- 1/4 tsp cumin seeds
- 1/8 tsp ground turmeric
- 1 large tomato, chopped
- 1 (16 oz.) package frozen sliced okra
- 1/4 tsp chili powder
- 1 tsp amchoor (mango powder), or juice of one lime
- salt to taste

Directions

- In a medium skillet, heat the oil on medium heat and sauté the mustard seeds till they begin to crackle.
- Stir in the asafoetida and reduce the heat to low.
- Stir in the onion, garlic, cumin seeds and turmeric and stir fry for about 5 minutes.
- Stir in the tomato and okra.
- Slowly, stir in the chili powder, amchoor and salt and cook for about 10 minutes.

Amount per serving 6

Timing Information:

Preparation	15 m
Cooking	15 m
Total Time	30 m

Nutritional Information:

Calories	146 kcal
Fat	12.5 g
Carbohydrates	8.6g
Protein	1.8 g
Cholesterol	0 mg
Sodium	6 mg

* Percent Daily Values are based on a 2,000 calorie diet.

Delish Indian Okra

Ingredients

- 2 tbsp vegetable oil
- 1 lb. small okra
- 1/2 tsp ground turmeric
- 1 clove garlic, chopped
- 1/2 tsp chopped fresh ginger
- 2 onions, cut into quarters
- 2 roma (plum) tomatoes, cut into quarters
- 1 tbsp chopped fresh cilantro

Directions

- In a large skillet, heat the oil on medium-high heat and sauté the okra for about 3 minutes.
- Transfer the okra into a plate.
- Sprinkle the turmeric into hot oil and heat for about 1-2 minutes.
- Add the garlic, ginger, onions and tomatoes and cook for about 10 minutes.
- Stir in the okra and remove from the heat.
- Serve with a garnishing of the cilantro.

Amount per serving 4

Timing Information:

Preparation	15 m
Cooking	15 m
Total Time	30 m

Nutritional Information:

Calories	125 kcal
Fat	7.1 g
Carbohydrates	14.8g
Protein	3.2 g
Cholesterol	0 mg
Sodium	13 mg

* Percent Daily Values are based on a 2,000 calorie diet.

Hearty Okra Soup

Ingredients

- 1 lb. ground beef
- 1/4 C. onion, chopped
- 1 (14.5 oz.) can diced tomatoes, drained
- 1 (14.5 oz.) can Italian diced tomatoes, drained
- 1 (16 oz.) package frozen mixed vegetables
- 1 C. sliced fresh or frozen okra
- 2 potatoes, peeled and chopped
- 1 tbsp ketchup
- salt and pepper to taste

Directions

- Heat a large skillet on medium heat and cook the ground beef and onion till the beef is browned completely.
- Drain the excess grease from the skillet.
- In a slow cooker, mix together the beef mixture, diced tomatoes, Italian diced tomatoes, vegetables, okra, potatoes, ketchup, salt, pepper and enough water to cover.
- Set the slow cooker on Low.
- Cook, covered for about 4 hours.

Amount per serving 4

Timing Information:

Preparation	20 m
Cooking	4 h
Total Time	4 h 20 m

Nutritional Information:

Calories	413 kcal
Fat	14 g
Carbohydrates	44.2g
Protein	27.3 g
Cholesterol	69 mg
Sodium	488 mg

* Percent Daily Values are based on a 2,000 calorie diet.

Red Café Stew

Ingredients

Roux:

- 1/2 C. all-purpose flour
- 1/2 C. vegetable oil

Vegetables:

- 1 tbsp butter
- 1 C. chopped celery
- 1 C. chopped green onions
- 1 green bell pepper, chopped

Tomato Sauce and Spices:

- 6 C. water
- 1 (8 oz.) can tomato sauce
- 2 tbsp Worcestershire sauce
- 2 cloves garlic, minced
- 2 tsp salt, or to taste
- 1 tsp hot pepper sauce (such as Tabasco(R))
- 1/2 tsp dried thyme

Seafood and Okra:

- 1 lb. frozen chopped okra
- 1 lb. catfish, cut into 2-inch pieces
- 1 1/2 lb. peeled and deveined shrimp

- 1 tbsp gumbo file powder
- 1/2 tsp salt

Directions

- For roux in a Dutch oven, mix together the vegetable oil and flour on medium-high heat and with a wooden spoon, cook for about 10 minutes, stirring continuously.
- Remove from the heat and keep aside to cool and thicken.
- In a skillet, melt the butter on medium heat and sauté the celery, green onions and bell pepper for about 10 minutes.
- Transfer the celery mixture into the pan with the roux and place on medium heat.
- Stir in the water, tomato sauce, Worcestershire sauce, garlic, and 2 tsp of the salt, hot pepper sauce and thyme and bring to a gentle boil.
- Reduce the heat to medium-low and simmer for about 1 hour.
- Stir in the okra and simmer for about 15 minutes.
- Gently, stir in the catfish and simmer for about 5 minutes.
- Gently stir in the shrimp and simmer for about 3 minutes.
- Stir in the file powder and salt and serve.

Amount per serving 8

Timing Information:

Preparation	25 m
Cooking	1 h 30 m
Total Time	1 h 55 m

Nutritional Information:

Calories	344 kcal
Fat	20.4 g
Carbohydrates	15.2g
Protein	25.4 g
Cholesterol	159 mg
Sodium	1129 mg

* Percent Daily Values are based on a 2,000 calorie diet.

Mango Prawns and Coconut Okra

Ingredients

- 1/2 lb. prawns, peeled and deveined
- sea salt to taste
- 1/2 C. grated coconut
- 4 chili peppers
- 1 tbsp coriander seeds
- 3 cloves garlic, peeled
- 5 peppercorns
- 1 tbsp vegetable oil
- 1 small onion, sliced
- 1/4 tsp ground turmeric
- 1 1/2 C. water, or as needed
- 3 oz. okra (bindhi), cut into thirds
- 3 pieces kokum (fruit from the mango family), or use mango

Directions

- Season the prawns with the sea salt.
- With a mortar and pestle, grind together the coconut, chili peppers, coriander seeds, garlic and peppercorns corns till the masala becomes orange evenly.

- In a pan, heat the oil on medium heat; cook and sauté the onion for about 5-10 minutes.
- Stir in the masala and turmeric and sauté for about 1 minute.
- Add enough water to make a smooth gravy and bring to a boil.
- Add the prawns and okra and cook for about 10 minutes.
- Stir in the kokum and again bring to a boil.
- Remove pot from heat and keep aside for some time before serving.

Amount per serving 6

Timing Information:

Preparation	10 m
Cooking	20 m
Total Time	30 m

Nutritional Information:

Calories	102 kcal
Fat	5.2 g
Carbohydrates	7.7g
Protein	7.2 g
Cholesterol	58 mg
Sodium	125 mg

* Percent Daily Values are based on a 2,000 calorie diet.

Rustic Road Tomato and Carrot Soup

Ingredients

- 2 tbsp olive oil
- 1/2 onion, chopped
- 3 stalks celery, chopped
- 2 cloves garlic, minced
- 4 C. vegetable broth
- 1 (15 oz.) can tomato sauce
- 4 carrots, peeled and cut into 1/4-inch rounds
- 2 baking potatoes, cut into bite-size pieces
- 1 C. frozen corn
- 1 C. frozen shelled edamame (green soybeans)
- 1 C. frozen sliced okra
- 2 leaves kale, roughly chopped
- salt to taste
- 1 tsp ground black pepper

Directions

- In a large pan, heat the oil on medium heat and sauté the onion and celery for about 5 minutes.
- Add the garlic and sauté for about 2-3 minutes.
- Add the vegetable broth and tomato sauce and simmer for about 10 minutes.

- Stir in the carrots and potatoes and simmer for about 10-15 minutes.
- Add the corn, edamame, okra and kale and simmer for about 5-10 minutes.
- Season with the salt and pepper and serve

Amount per serving 10

Timing Information:

Preparation	15 m
Cooking	35 m
Total Time	50 m

Nutritional Information:

Calories	151 kcal
Fat	5 g
Carbohydrates	22.5g
Protein	6.4 g
Cholesterol	0 mg
Sodium	440 mg

* Percent Daily Values are based on a 2,000 calorie diet.

Complex Mutton Stew

Ingredients

- 5 lb. bone-in mutton shoulder or leg, cut into 1 lb. pieces
- 2 tsp salt
- 1 tbsp Italian seasoning
- 3 lb. baking potatoes, peeled and cubed
- 1 lb. carrots, peeled and sliced
- 2 (15 oz.) cans crushed tomatoes
- 2 tsp canola oil
- 1 small onion, chopped
- 2 C. medium salsa
- 1 (15 oz.) can tomato sauce
- 1/2 C. packed brown sugar
- 1/4 C. hickory smoke flavored barbeque sauce
- 1 (15.25 oz.) can whole kernel corn, drained
- 1 (14.5 oz.) can green beans, drained
- 1 (16 oz.) package frozen lima beans, thawed
- 1 (10 oz.) package frozen okra
- 1 (46 fluid oz.) can tomato juice

Directions

- 1st day: In a large heavy soup pan, add meat, 1 tsp of the salt, Italian seasoning and enough water to cover on medium heat and simmer for about 1 hour.

- Set your oven to 375 degrees F.
- Remove from the heat and with a slotted spoon transfer the meat into a bowl.
- Refrigerate the stock for later use.
- Remove the meat from the bones and discard the bones.
- In a roasting pan, place the meat and cook in the oven for about 1 1/2 hours.
- With a piece of foil, cover the roasting pan and refrigerate.
- 2nd day: Remove the stock from the refrigerator.
- With a spoon, skim off the top layer of hardened white fat and discard.
- In a heavy soup pan, add 4 C. of the stock, potatoes, carrots, 1 can of the crushed tomatoes and 1 tsp of the salt on medium-high heat and cook for about 20 minutes, stirring occasionally.
- Remove from the heat and keep aside to cool slightly before placing in the refrigerator.
- Set your oven to 300 degrees F.
- In a small skillet, heat the olive oil on medium heat and sauté the onion for about 5-8 minutes.
- Remove from the heat and keep aside.
- Remove the roasting pan of meat from the refrigerator and add in the remaining stock.
- With a piece of foil, cover the roasting pan and cook in the oven for about 1 1/2 hours.

- Remove the roasting pan from the oven and stir in the salsa, onion, tomato sauce, brown sugar, barbecue sauce and 1 can crushed tomatoes.
- Cook in the oven for about 1 1/2 hours.
- Remove from the oven and keep aside to cool slightly before placing in the refrigerator for overnight.
- 3rd day: Set your oven to 300 degrees F.
- In a large Dutch oven, mix together the meat, vegetable mixture from the day before, corn, green beans, lima beans, okra and tomato juice.
- Cook in the oven for about 3 hours, stirring occasionally.

Amount per serving 20

Timing Information:

Preparation	1 h 10 m
Cooking	9 h 10 m
Total Time	2 d 10 h 20 m

Nutritional Information:

Calories	532 kcal
Fat	25.6 g
Carbohydrates	49.7g
Protein	28.2 g
Cholesterol	82 mg
Sodium	975 mg

* Percent Daily Values are based on a 2,000 calorie diet.

Egyptian Dinner

Ingredients

- 1/4 C. olive oil
- 1 large onion, finely chopped
- 1 lb. boneless lamb shoulder, cut into 1-inch pieces
- salt and ground black pepper to taste
- 1 (8 oz.) can tomato sauce
- 2 C. water
- 1 (10 oz.) package frozen okra, thawed

Directions

- In a large pan, melt the butter on medium heat and sauté the onion for about 7 minutes.
- Add the lamb, salt, and black pepper and stir fry for about 5-10 minutes.
- Stir in the tomato sauce, water, salt and black pepper and bring to a boil.
- Reduce the heat to low and simmer, stirring occasionally for about 1 hour, adding more water if required.
- Set your oven to 350 degrees F.
- In the pan, stir in the okra and more water if required and bring to a boil.

- Stir in the salt and black pepper and transfer everything into a 2-quart baking dish.
- Cover the baking dish with a piece of the foil and cook in the oven for about 35 minutes.
- Remove the piece of the foil and cook in the oven for about 10 minutes more.

Amount per serving 4

Timing Information:

Preparation	15 m
Cooking	2 h
Total Time	2 h 15 m

Nutritional Information:

Calories	339 kcal
Fat	25.7 g
Carbohydrates	11.2g
Protein	16.9 g
Cholesterol	58 mg
Sodium	337 mg

* Percent Daily Values are based on a 2,000 calorie diet.

Asian Dream Okra Stir Fry

Ingredients

- 2 tbsp olive oil
- 1/2 bell pepper, seeded and sliced into strips
- 2 jalapeno peppers, seeded and sliced into strips
- 1 tbsp minced fresh ginger root
- 1 tbsp minced garlic
- 2 bay leaves
- 1 tsp ground coriander
- 1/2 tsp ground red pepper
- 1/4 tsp ground turmeric
- 1/4 tsp cumin seeds
- 1/8 tsp ground cardamom
- 1/8 tsp ground black pepper
- 1/8 tsp ground cinnamon
- 1 small tomato, sliced
- 1/4 C. golden raisins
- 1 C. sliced okra
- 1 C. coconut milk
- 1 tbsp water
- salt to taste

Directions

- In a large skillet, heat the oil and sauté the bell pepper for about 3 minutes.
- Stir in the jalapeño peppers, ginger, garlic and bay leaves into the bell pepper and sauté for about 2-3 minutes.

- Stir in the coriander, red pepper, turmeric, cumin seeds, cardamom, black pepper and cinnamon and sauté for about 2 minutes.
- Stir in the tomato slices and raisins and cook for about 3 minutes.
- Add the okra and stir to coat with the spices completely.
- In a bowl, mix together the coconut milk and water.
- Add the coconut milk mixture into the skillet and cook, covered for about 8-10 minutes.
- Add the water if required to keep moist.
- Season with the salt and serve warm.

Amount per serving 2

Timing Information:

Preparation	15 m
Cooking	20 m
Total Time	35 m

Nutritional Information:

Calories	456 kcal
Fat	38.4 g
Carbohydrates	30.5g
Protein	5.5 g
Cholesterol	0 mg
Sodium	27 mg

* Percent Daily Values are based on a 2,000 calorie diet.

Jamaican Veggie Stew

Ingredients

- 1 C. uncooked brown rice
- water
- 1/2 lb. collard greens, chopped
- 2 cloves garlic, peeled
- 1 (10 oz.) package frozen okra
- 1 (28 oz.) can whole peeled tomatoes, chopped, with liquid
- 1 chayote squash, diced
- 2 cloves garlic, crushed
- 1/4 tsp ground ginger
- 1/4 tsp dried dill weed
- 1/4 tsp ground cumin
- 1 tbsp chopped fresh cilantro
- 1 (16 oz.) can kidney beans, rinsed and drained
- 1 (6 oz.) can tomato paste
- all-purpose flour, as needed

Directions

- In a pan, add the brown rice and water on high heat and bring to a boil.
- Reduce the heat to medium-low and simmer, covered for about 45-50 minutes.

- In a pan, place the collard greens, 2 peeled whole garlic cloves and enough water to cover and boil for about 15 minutes.
- Drain well.
- In another large pan, add the okra, tomatoes, chayote squash and 2 crushed garlic cloves and bring to a boil.
- Cook for about 5 minutes.
- Reduce to a simmer and stir in the collard greens, ground ginger, dill weed, ground cumin and cilantro and simmer for about 40-60 minutes.
- In a bowl, add the kidney beans and tomato paste and mash well.
- In the pan, add the mashed beans mixture and cooked rice and mix well.
- Stir in a spoonful of flour to thicken.
- Adjust the seasonings to taste.

Amount per serving 6

Timing Information:

Preparation	30 m
Cooking	1 h 40 m
Total Time	2 h 10 m

Nutritional Information:

Calories	235 kcal
Fat	1.5 g
Carbohydrates	48.8g
Protein	10.5 g
Cholesterol	0 mg
Sodium	218 mg

* Percent Daily Values are based on a 2,000 calorie diet.

Old-Fashioned Middle-Eastern Stew

Ingredients

- 2 tbsp extra-virgin olive oil
- 1/4 C. crushed garlic
- 2 lb. cubed leg of lamb meat
- 1 tsp ground cumin
- 1 tsp chopped fresh mint
- 1 tsp ground dried turmeric
- 1 tsp chopped fresh rosemary
- 2 (14.5 oz.) cans diced tomatoes, drained
- 2 tbsp tomato paste
- 1 lb. baby okra
- 1 tsp lemon juice
- 1 C. water
- 1 tbsp butter
- 1 C. thin egg noodles
- 2 C. long grain rice
- 2 C. chicken broth
- 2 C. water
- 1 pinch salt and pepper to taste
- 1 tsp olive oil

Directions

- In a large skillet, heat the olive oil on medium heat and sauté the garlic till transparent.
- Add the cubed lamb and sear till browned from all sides.

- Season with the cumin, mint, turmeric and rosemary and cook for about 5 minutes.
- Stir in the diced tomatoes, tomato paste, okra, lemon juice and water and reduce the heat to low.
- Simmer, covered for about 45 minutes.
- Meanwhile in a pan, melt the butter on medium heat and sauté the egg noodles till toasted.
- Add the chicken broth and water and bring to a boil.
- Stir in the rice and reduce the heat to low.
- Simmer, covered for about 15 minutes.
- Stir the salt, pepper and olive oil before serving.
- Serve the lamb stew over the rice pilaf.

Amount per serving 6

Timing Information:

Preparation	20 m
Cooking	45 m
Total Time	1 h 5 m

Nutritional Information:

Calories	552 kcal
Fat	19.1 g
Carbohydrates	67g
Protein	25.5 g
Cholesterol	72 mg
Sodium	325 mg

* Percent Daily Values are based on a 2,000 calorie diet.

A Filipino Dinner

Ingredients

- 2 (8 oz.) fillets milkfish (bangus)
- 1 tomato, quartered
- 1 onion, chopped
- 2 tbsp shrimp paste (bagoong)
- 1 C. water
- salt and pepper to taste
- 1/2 lb. long beans, cut into bite-size pieces
- 1/2 lb. zucchini, cut into bite-size pieces
- 1/2 lb. fresh okra

Directions

- Set your outdoor grill for medium-high heat and lightly, grease the grill grate.
- Cook the milkfish fillets on the grill for about 2-3 minutes from both sides.
- In a pan, mix together the grilled fillets, tomato, onion, shrimp paste on medium-high heat and water and bring to a boil for about 5 minutes.
- Season with the salt and pepper and reduce the heat to medium.

- Stir in the long beans and zucchini and cook for about 5 minutes.
- Stir in the okra and cook for about 5 minutes.
- Serve hot.

Amount per serving 6

Timing Information:

Preparation	30 m
Cooking	20 m
Total Time	50 m

Nutritional Information:

Calories	288 kcal
Fat	5.8 g
Carbohydrates	32.7g
Protein	27.5 g
Cholesterol	43 mg
Sodium	140 mg

* Percent Daily Values are based on a 2,000 calorie diet.

Okra Veggie Combo

Ingredients

- 1 C. oil for frying
- 2 C. okra, cut into bite-size pieces
- 2 tbsp vegetable oil
- 1 C. diced onion
- 1 tsp salt
- 1 green chili pepper, chopped
- 1/2 tsp ginger paste
- 1/2 tsp garlic paste
- 1 pinch ground turmeric
- 1 C. diced fresh tomatoes
- 2 tsp ground coriander
- 2 tsp ground cumin
- 1/2 tsp cayenne powder
- 2 C. chopped bell peppers (yellow, green, red)
- 1 C. chopped fresh cilantro
- 1/2 tsp garam masala

Directions

- In a skillet, heat about 1-inch of the oil on medium heat and fry the okra for about 2-3 minutes.
- Transfer the fried okra onto a paper towel-lined plate to drain.
- In another skillet, heat 2 tbsp of the oil and sauté the onion and salt for about 5-10 minutes.

- Add the green chili pepper, ginger paste, garlic paste and turmeric and sauté for about 1 minute.
- Stir in the tomatoes and cook for about 2 minutes.
- Stir in the ground coriander, ground cumin and cayenne powder and sauté for about 4 minutes.
- Stir in the bell peppers and cilantro and cook for about 2 minutes.
- Stir in the okra and reduce the heat to very low.
- Simmer for about 4 minutes.
- Serve with a sprinkling of the garam masala.

Amount per serving 4

Timing Information:

Preparation	15 m
Cooking	20 m
Total Time	35 m

Nutritional Information:

Calories	186 kcal
Fat	13.3 g
Carbohydrates	15.9g
Protein	3.4 g
Cholesterol	0 mg
Sodium	622 mg

* Percent Daily Values are based on a 2,000 calorie diet.

STUFFED OKRA SAMPLER

Ingredients

- 2 tbsp mango powder (amchoor)
- 1 tsp ground ginger
- 1 tsp ground cumin
- 1 tsp ground turmeric
- 1/2 tsp chili powder (optional)
- 1/2 tsp salt
- 1/2 tsp vegetable oil
- 1 lb. large okra
- 1/4 C. corn flour
- vegetable oil for frying

Directions

- In a bowl, mix together the mango powder, ginger, cumin, turmeric, chili powder, salt and 1/2 tsp of the oil and keep aside for about 2 hours.
- In a large pan, heat the vegetable oil to 350 degrees F.
- Trim the okra and make a slit lengthwise down the side of each okra, creating a pocket.
- Stuff each pocket with the spice mixture.
- In a resealable plastic bag; place the corn flour.
- Add the stuffed okra and shake to coat well.
- Fry the okra in the hot oil for about 5-8 minutes.
- With a slotted spoon, transfer the fried okra onto a paper towel-lined plate to drain.

Amount per serving 4

Timing Information:

Preparation	15 m
Cooking	5 m
Total Time	2 h 20 m

Nutritional Information:

Calories	200 kcal
Fat	12.2 g
Carbohydrates	22.3g
Protein	3.2 g
Cholesterol	0 mg
Sodium	307 mg

* Percent Daily Values are based on a 2,000 calorie diet.

Thanks for Reading! Join the Club and Keep on Cooking with 6 More Cookbooks....

http://bit.ly/1TdrStv

To grab the box sets simply follow the link mentioned above, or tap one of book covers.

This will take you to a page where you can simply enter your email address and a PDF version of the box sets will be emailed to you.

Hope you are ready for some serious cooking!

http://bit.ly/1TdrStv

Come On...
Let's Be Friends :)

We adore our readers and love connecting with them socially.

Like BookSumo on Facebook and let's get social!

Facebook

And also check out the BookSumo Cooking Blog.

Food Lover Blog

Printed in Great Britain
by Amazon